Open Sesame Vegetable Juice

4 carrots, about 400g/14oz in weight
115g/4oz/¾ cup green beans (string
   beans), trimmed
1 tbsp tahini
Few toasted sesame seeds

1 Feed the carrots and beans through a juicer.

2 Stir in the tahini until well combined. If it is too thick, thin it with a little warm water before adding it to the juice.

3 Pour into glasses and sprinkle with sesame seeds.

Meal in One: If serving as a meal substitute, whisk in some soft tofu to provide protein.

Sesame seeds contain valuable nutrients, particularly calcium, which strengthens bones, as well as iron, vitamin E, and protein. Tahini is made from sesame seeds ground to a paste.

Winter Winner

1 large parsnip, trimmed
2 carrots, trimmed
Small handful coriander (cilantro)
1 small bulb fennel, cut into chunks
2 crisp green apples, quartered

1 Feed the parsnips and carrots through the juicer.

2 Feed the coriander (cilantro) through the juicer, followed by the fennel and apple.

3 Pour into glasses and serve.

Winter Winner Basilico: Use basil in place of the coriander.

Celery Winner: Replace the fennel with 4 or 5 sticks of celery.

keep yourself strong

Smokin' Red Pepper Juice

2 red peppers, seeded and cut
   into strips
1 large courgette (zucchini)
1 clove garlic
1 orange, peeled and segmented
½ tsp smoked paprika

1 Feed the pepper, courgette (zucchini), garlic, and orange segments through a juicer.

2 Stir in the smoked paprika and serve.

Sunny Smokin' Pepper Juice: Use yellow or orange peppers in place of the red pepper.

Rosy Smokin' Pepper Juice: Add 1 medium ripe tomato.

Totally Tropical Juice

½ mango, peeled and cut into chunks
¼ papaya, seeded, peeled, and cut
  into chunks
1 wedge pineapple, peeled and cut
  into chunks
1 kiwi fruit, peeled and cut
  into wedges
1 banana, peeled
1 passion fruit
1–2 slices star fruit (optional)

1 Feed the first five fruits through
a juicer in the order listed.

2 Pour into a glass.

3 Cut the passion fruit in half,
scoop out the seeds, and stir
  into the juice.

4 Decorate the glass with the star
  fruit if desired.

Totally Tropical Smoothie: All the fruit
can be placed in a blender for
a super thick smoothie.

Carrot, Beetroot, and Ginger Juice

2 large carrots, trimmed
1cm/½ inch piece of ginger root, peeled
1 beetroot (beet), washed and trimmed

1 Feed the carrots, ginger, and then the beetroot (beet) through a juicer.

2 Serve well chilled.

Carrot, Beetroot, and Celery Juice:
Replace the ginger with 2 sticks of celery.

tame your tummy

Chilli Mango and Lime Smoothie

1 ripe mango, peeled, stoned and cut into chunks
2 limes
1 small red chilli, seeded and chopped
Few fresh mint leaves

1 Place the mango in a blender.

2 Squeeze the juice from the limes and add to the blender. Then add the chilli.

3 Blend until smooth.

4 Pour into a glass and top with a few small mint leaves.

Minty Mango and Lime Smoothie:
Replace the chilli with a few fresh mint leaves.

Waldorf Juice

4 sticks celery, cut into short lengths
2 tbsp raisins
1 tbsp walnuts
1 crisp apple, cut into wedges
1 tbsp low-fat fromage frais (yogurt) or
    crème fraîche (optional)
Celery sticks to stir

1 Feed the celery, raisins, walnuts, and apple through the juicer.

2 Serve topped with the fromage frais (yogurt) or crème fraîche and a celery stick to stir.

Sweet Waldorf Juice: Add a carrot for a slightly sweeter juice.

Cardamom is an aid to digestion, and it is also thought to help battle colds, fevers, inflammatory conditions, and liver problems. Ricotta cheese is a good source of calcium.

Creamy Orange Delight

3 cardamom pods
115g/4oz/⅛ cup ricotta cheese
225ml/8floz/1 cup freshly squeezed
orange juice
1–2 tsp clear honey

1 Remove the seeds from the cardamom pods and grind in a pestle and mortar.

2 Place in a blender with the ricotta cheese and blend.

3 With the motor running, gradually pour in the orange juice.

4 Sweeten with honey and serve over ice if desired.

Pumpkin Pie Smoothie

150g/5oz/1¼ cups pumpkin flesh,
  cubed
¼ tsp ground cinnamon
Pinch grated nutmeg
1 small red chilli, seeded and chopped
225ml/8floz/1 cup orange juice

1 Steam the pumpkin for 10 minutes until just tender and let cool.

2 Place in a blender with the remaining ingredients. Blend until smooth.

3 Chill well and serve cold.

Spicy Squash Smoothie: Use a butternut squash instead of the pumpkin.

Cool Avocado Angel

1 avocado, peeled and stoned
½ cucumber, peeled and cut into
  chunks
225ml/8floz/1cup orange juice

1 Place all the ingredients in a blender and blend until smooth.

2 Pour into glasses half-filled with ice and serve.

Avocado Devil: Add 1 seeded, chopped red chilli to the mix to spice up the smoothie.

A super-charged avocado adds thickness to this smoothie. Avocado is an excellent source of potassium, folic acid (folate), and vitamin A, as well as protein, iron, and other vitamins and minerals.

sing from the heart

Deep Purple Smoothie

115g/4oz/¾ cup black or green grapes
115g/4oz/1 cup cherries, pitted
125ml/4floz/½ cup cranberry juice
Few cherries to serve

1 Feed the grapes through a juicer.

2 Add the grape juice, cherries, and cranberry juice to a blender and blend until smooth.

3 Pour over ice in glasses, decorate with a few cherries, and serve.

Nutty Banana Smoothie

1 banana
225ml/8floz/1 cup milk
1 tbsp smooth peanut butter

1 Peel and slice the banana, wrap it in clingfilm (plastic wrap), and freeze overnight.

2 Place all the ingredients in a blender and blend until smooth.

3 Pour in a glass and serve immediately.

Banana and Sesame Smoothie:
Instead of peanut butter use 2 tsp tahini.

Health in a Glass

2 medium tomatoes
210g/7½oz/3 cups cabbage,
    thickly shredded
Handful of parsley
Celery stick to serve

1 Feed the tomatoes, cabbage, and parsley through a juicer.

2 Pour into a glass and add a celery stick before serving.

Liquorice Liquor: Replace the parsley with 1 small bulb of fennel, cut into chunks.

Spinach is a good source of **folic acid** (folate), which is especially important for pregnant women. The tomatoes provide vitamin C, which helps to unlock the iron and calcium in spinach.

Green Giant Juice

2 medium tomatoes
150g/5oz/1¾ cups broccoli
150g/5oz/3 cups spinach

1 Cut a few slices from the tomato and reserve. Feed the tomatoes, broccoli, and spinach through a juicer.

2 Pour over ice in glasses and decorate with the tomato slices before serving.

Spiced Green Giant Juice: Add a pinch of grated nutmeg for some spice.

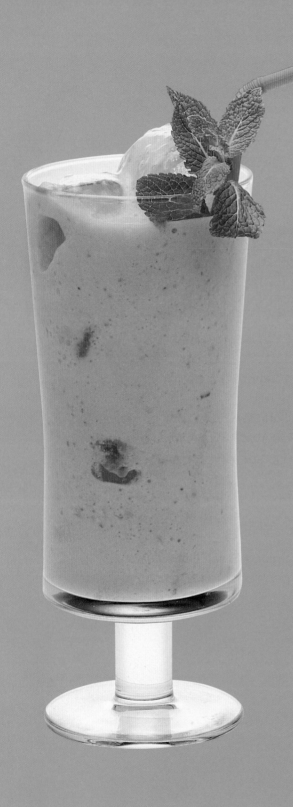

Strawberry and Mint Smoothie

115g/4oz/1 cup strawberries, washed
  and hulled
225ml/8floz/1 cup soy milk
85g/3oz/⅓ cup firm tofu
10 mint leaves, chopped
Mint leaves to decorate

1 Place all the strawberries, soy milk, and tofu in a blender. Add the chopped mint and blend until smooth. If the smoothies are too thick, stir in a little extra soy milk.

2 Pour into tall glasses and decorate with whole mint leaves to serve.

Raspberry and Mint Smoothie: Use raspberries instead of strawberries.

Blackberry and Mint Smoothie: Use blackberries instead of strawberries.

Creamy Borscht

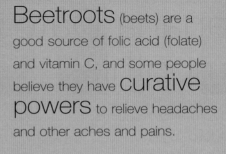

3 small beetroots (beets)
4 spring onions (scallions), trimmed
2 tsp lemon juice
85ml/3floz/¾ cup fromage frais (yogurt)
   or double (heavy) cream
Few chives, snipped

1 Feed the beetroots (beets) and onions (scallions) through a juicer.

2 Stir in the lemon juice and fromage frais (yogurt) or cream.

3 Pour into glasses and sprinkle with the snipped chives.

Borscht with a Kick: Add 1 tbsp dry sherry to the juice.

Slim 'n' Creamy Borscht: Use low-fat fromage frais or low-fat natural (plain) yogurt instead of the regular fromage frais or cream.

Beetroots (beets) are a good source of folic acid (folate) and vitamin C, and some people believe they have curative powers to relieve headaches and other aches and pains.

Banana Date Smoothie

125ml/4floz/½ cup milk
4 tbsp yogurt
1 tbsp date syrup
1 banana, peeled
4 dates, stoned and chopped
2 tsp wheat germ

1 Place all the ingredients in a blender and blend until smooth.

2 Pour into a glass and serve.

Dairy-free Banana Date Smoothie:
Use soy milk to replace the milk and yogurt for a dairy-free smoothie.

Wheat germ contains valuable B vitamins. Date syrup is a great way to add sweetness without adding sugar.

Gazpacho Smoothie

¼ red pepper
¼ green pepper
¼ red onion, peeled
¼ cucumber
1 clove garlic
Few sprigs parsley
1 tsp red wine vinegar
225ml/8floz/1 cup tomato juice
5 tbsp cold water
Dash Tabasco sauce
Freshly ground black pepper
Cucumber and parsley to decorate

1 Place all the ingredients in a blender and blend until smooth.

2 Serve chilled, decorated with slices of cucumber and a few parsley leaves.

The most colorful peppers provide the most **bioflavonoids**, which may help prevent cancer. Red peppers have more antioxidants than green peppers, but green peppers have more vitamin C than red peppers.

Lemongrass and Lime Smoothie

1 stick lemongrass
1 lime
2 tsp wheat germ
225ml/8floz/1cup whole-milk yogurt
1–2 tsp clear honey

1 Trim the ends of the lemon grass and remove the tough outer layers. Thinly slice the remainder; place in a blender.

2 Grate the zest from the lime and squeeze the juice. Add the zest and juice to the blender and blend until the lemon grass is finely chopped.

3 Add the wheat germ, yogurt, and honey and blend until smooth.

Lemongrass and Orange Smoothie: For a sweeter smoothie, replace the lime with 1 orange or 2 tangerines.

Peach and Almond Smoothie

2 peaches, stoned
2 tbsp toasted flaked almonds
225ml/8floz/1 cup freshly squeezed orange juice

1 Place the peaches and almonds in a blender and blend until smooth.

2 Add the orange juice and blend again.

3 Pour into glasses to serve.

Peach and Cashew Smoothie: Use lightly toasted cashew nuts instead of the almonds.

Peach and Hazelnut Smoothie: Use lightly toasted hazelnuts instead of the almonds.

 Wheat germ is packed full of calcium, and it has the B vitamins, vitamin E, magnesium, iron, and zinc, making this a nutritious ingredient.

Red Slaw Juice

½ small red cabbage, thickly shredded

1 carrot, trimmed

1 tbsp seedless raisins

2 apples, quartered

1 tbsp lemon juice

1 Feed the cabbage, carrot, raisins, and apples through a juicer.

2 Stir in the lemon juice and serve.

Nutty Slaw Juice: Grind a few shelled walnuts and add to the juice.

Fig and Apricot Smoothie

3 large figs, trimmed and quartered

4 apricots, stoned

1 tbsp wheat germ or oatmeal

125ml/4floz/½ cup freshly squeezed orange juice

1 tbsp lemon juice, freshly squeezed

1 Place all the ingredients in a blender and blend until smooth.

2 Pour into glasses and serve.

Fig and Date Smoothie: Replace the apricots with fresh pitted dates.

keep your tummy happy

Lime and Passion Fruit Cooler

1 lime
4 passion fruit
125ml/4floz/½ cup apple juice

1 Grate the zest from one lime and place in a blender. Cut the pith and peel away from the lime, then add the flesh to the blender.

2 Scoop out the passion fruit seeds into the blender, add the apple juice, and blend briefly.

3 Strain through a nylon sieve, pour into a glass, and serve.

Orange and Passion Fruit Cooler: Replace lime zest with orange zest and replace the apple juice with orange juice.

Tofu Cooler: Add 115g/4oz/½ cup silken tofu with the apple juice.

Carrot, Apple, and Ginger Juice

2 large carrots, trimmed and cut
   into chunks
2 apples, quartered
1cm/½ inch piece of ginger root, peeled
Carrot sticks to serve

1 Feed the carrot, apple, and ginger
through a juicer.

2 Pour into glasses, add carrot sticks to
stir, and serve.

Carrot, Apple, and Chilli Juice:
Replace the ginger with a small seeded
chilli for a real zip.

Ginger can help to relieve
nausea and morning sickness.

Pear and Choc Hazelnut Shake

1 soft ripe pear, peeled and cored
2 tbsp chocolate hazelnut spread or
  chocolate spread
225ml/8floz/1 cup milk
Vanilla or chocolate ice cream (optional)

1 Place the pear, chocolate hazelnut spread, and milk in a blender and blend until smooth and frothy.

2 Pour into glasses and add a scoop of ice cream if desired.

Peach and Choc Hazelnut Shake:
Use one peach in place of the pear.

Banana and Choc Hazelnut Shake:
Replace the pear with a peeled banana.

Keep this for the occasional treat because it has a high-fat content. However, peanuts are a good source of potassium and folic acid (folate). Nuts are a rich source of vitamin E, used to make red blood cells.

Chocolate and Peanut Butter Shake

2 tbsp cocoa powder
50g/2oz plain (dark) chocolate, broken
  into chunks
2 tbsp smooth peanut butter
350ml/12floz/1½ cups milk

1 Place the cocoa powder in a heatproof bowl with the chocolate, peanut butter, and 3 tbsp of the milk.

2 Place over a pan of hot water and heat gently, stirring until the chocolate melts and the ingredients combine. Let cool.

3 Place in a blender and, with the motor running, slowly add the remaining milk.

Choc-and-Peanut Ice Cream Shake:
Place a small scoop of chocolate ice cream and one small scoop of vanilla ice cream in the glasses and pour the shake over the ice cream.

Rose and Strawberry Milk

15g/½oz scented rose petals,
    washed well, or 1 tbsp rosewater
300ml/10oz/1¼ cups milk
85g/3oz/¾ cup strawberries, washed
    and hulled

1 Place the rose petals in a small pan with half the milk and bring to a simmer. Remove from the heat and let cool. If you are using rosewater instead, simply add to the milk without heating.

2 Pour into a blender, add the strawberries, and blend until smooth.

3 Add the remaining milk and blend again. Chill before serving.

Rose and Raspberry Milk: Use raspberries in place of the strawberries.

Iced Coffee Shake

225ml/8floz/1 cup strong black coffee
2 tbsp demerara sugar (light brown
    sugar)
225ml/8floz/1 cup cold milk
4 tbsp single (light) or double (heavy)
    cream

1 Stir the sugar into a cup of freshly made black coffee and let cool.

2 Stir in the milk. Pour into a shallow freezer container and freeze for about 2–4 hours until slushy.

3 Scoop into a blender, add the cream, and blend to break up the ice crystals. Serve immediately.

Extra-Rich Iced Coffee Shake:
Add 2 scoops of vanilla ice cream to the blender.

make me feel happy

Carrot and Spinach Zing

6 carrots, trimmed
115g/4oz/1 cup spinach leaves
2.5cm/1 inch piece of ginger root, peeled
1 tsp Klamath blue green algae (optional)

1 Feed the carrots, spinach, and ginger through a juicer.

2 Stir in the Klamath blue green algae if using and serve over ice.

Carrot and Rocket Zing: Use rocket (arugula) in place of the spinach.

Carrot and Watercress Zing: Use watercress in place of the spinach.

Slimmer's Lassi

1 mango, stoned
225ml/8floz/1 cup low-fat natural (plain) yogurt
125ml/4floz/½ cup skimmed milk
Crushed ice

1 Place the mango, yogurt, and milk in a blender and blend until smooth.

2 Pour over crushed ice to serve.

Slimmer's Banana Lassi: Replace the mango with 1 large, ripe peeled banana.

Slimmer's Berry Lassi: Instead of the mango, use 115g/4oz/¾–1 cup of fresh berries.

Klamath blue green algae is packed with protein and minerals that are good for the body. It helps stop food cravings, which makes it ideal when dieting.

Cucumber is a good **diuretic,** so it can help stop water retention and aid weight loss. Cucumber also helps to lower blood pressure.

Melon and Cucumber Cooler

½ small honeydew melon, peeled, seeded, and cut into chunks
½ cucumber
Sparkling mineral water (optional)

1 Place the melon and cucumber in a blender and blend until smooth.

2 Pour into glasses.

3 Dilute with sparkling mineral water if required.

Melon, Cucumber, and Celery Cooler: Add 2 sticks of celery.

Watermelon and Orange Smoothie

450g/1lb/3 cups watermelon, peeled and cut into chunks
4 oranges

1 Discard most of the seeds and place the watermelon in a blender.

2 Squeeze the juice from the oranges and add to the blender.

3 Blend until smooth and serve over ice.

Watermelon and Lemon Smoothie: Instead of 4 oranges use 2 oranges and 2 lemons for a tangier flavor.

Melon and Orange Smoothie: Use honeydew, canteloupe, or another variety of melon instead of watermelon.

vitamin-packed

Grapes and berries contain sulphur, which is good for **healthy skin**.

24 •

Grape and Raspberry Glow

225ml/8floz/1cup red grape juice
175g/6oz/1½ cups raspberries

1 Place the fruit in a blender, reserving a few raspberries. Blend until well combined.

2 Push through a nylon sieve to remove seeds if desired.

3 Pour into a glass and top with reserved raspberries.

Green Grapes and Blueberry Glow:
Substitute the ingredients with seedless green grapes and blueberries.

Pineapple has one of the strongest protein-digesting enzymes, bromelain, and melons have diuretic and digestive cleansing properties, making this drink ideal for improving your digestive system and helping to alleviate digestive problems.

Melon, Pineapple, and Mango Smoothie

1 wedge cantaloupe melon, peeled and cut into chunks
1 wedge pineapple, peeled and cut into chunks
½ mango, peeled and cut into chunks
125ml/4floz/½ cup freshly squeezed orange juice
Mango slices to decorate

1 Place all the ingredients in a blender and blend until smooth.

2 Pour over ice, if desired, and decorate with slices of mango.

Fruity Juice: Feed the ingredients through a juicer for a thinner juice drink.

Papaya, Pineapple, and Mango Smoothie: Give the drink even more protein-digesting enzymes by adding a wedge of papaya to the mix.

Making Simple Juices

Some recipes for smoothies require the addition of fruit juices. You can use shop-bought juices, but if you have a juicer, you may want to make your own fresh juice for your smoothies, or you may simply want to make single fruit juices to drink. Here is a guide to how much juice you will get from the most popular fruit and vegetables.

To make 225ml/8floz/1 cup you will need:

Apple Juice: 4–5 apples
Orange Juice: 3–4 oranges
Pineapple Juice: ½ medium --pineapple
Tomato Juice: 4–6 medium tomatoes
Carrot Juice: 5–6 large carrots
Grapefruit Juice: 2 grapefruit
Grape Juice: 225–300g/8–10oz/
   2–2½ cups grapes
Mango Juice: 1½–2 mangoes
Pear Juice: 4–5 pears
Cherry Juice: 450–500g/1lb–1lb2oz/
   2–2½ cups cherries
Pomegranate Juice: 4–5 pomegranates

Use these quantities only as a guide. These juices were made using a centrifugal juicer (see pages 16–17). If you use a masticating juicer, you will get a larger quantity of juice because these machines are more efficient. Also remember that the amount of juice will vary between the different varieties of the same fruit and even from season to season. Ripe local fruits in season are usually juicier than fruits that have been picked unripe and flown across the world.

Juices Hints and Tips

Recipes make one to two glasses, depending on the size of your glass and the amount you want to drink. In general, vegetable juices are drunk in smaller quantities than fruit juices.

Stick to one type of measuring system. Never switch between them. Cup measurements are for standard American cups.

Always use fruit and vegetables that are in peak condition.

Wash fruit and vegetables well before use.

Prepare fruit and vegetables just before you need them. Some vitamins will start to be destroyed when you cut into the produce, and some fruit and vegetables discolor quickly.

Use organic ingredients if you want to avoid pesticide residues.

Cut vegetables into pieces that can be fed through the juicer's feeding tube easily. This will vary from machine to machine. Some machines will take whole apples, others will need the fruit or vegetables to be cut up in small pieces.

Insert soft fruit such as strawberries and blueberries slowly to extract the most juice. Follow soft fruit and leaves with a harder fruit such as an apple or a vegetable.

If you do need to store the juice, keep it in the refrigerator and add a few drops of lemon juice. (This will keep it from discoloring.)

Serve well chilled – use chilled vegetables and fruit or serve over ice.

Dilute juices for children with an equal quantity of water. You can use sparkling mineral water to create a fizzy fruit drink.

Fruit is high in fructose, a natural sugar, so people with diabetes should not drink too much. Dilute with water if necessary.

Do not drink more than 3 glasses of juice a day unless you are used to it – too much juice can cause an upset stomach.

Very dark vegetables such as beetroot (beet) and broccoli can have strong flavors. Dilute with water or with a milder flavored juice such as apple or celery if you want.

Smoothie Bases

Many smoothies are 100 percent fruit, but to blend efficiently a liquid is often added.

Fruit juice: In 100 percent fruit smoothies, fruit juice is added if necessary. If you have a juicer, juice your own fruit to maximize the vitamin content (see pages 12–13). For speed or convenience, you can use shop-brought juices. Chilled juices not made from concentrate have the best flavor.

Yogurt: When yogurt is added as a base it adds valuable calcium to the smoothie. Using a yogurt with live bacteria is good for the digestion, providing healthy bacteria. Greek-style yogurt will give the creamiest results but has the highest calorie content. Whole-milk yogurt can be used as a substitute for Greek-style yogurt. It adds more creaminess to the drink than a low-fat yogurt, with a calorie content that is higher than low-fat yogurt but not as high as Greek-style yogurt. Fruit-flavored yogurt may have a lot of added sugar.

Milk: Like yogurt, milk added to smoothies provides a good source of calcium. Calcium is important for growing children, and smoothies are a good way of including milk in a fussy child's diet. Whole-fat milk has the most flavor, but for those wishing to reduce fat content, skimmed or semi-skimmed milk is better.

Cream: For special occasions, adding single (light) or double (heavy) cream to a smoothie will give it a richer flavor.

Crème fraîche, fromage frais, quark, cottage cheese, mascarpone: These dairy products can be added to smoothies to provide calcium and as thickeners. The fat content varies and those with a high-fat content such as full-fat crème fraîche and mascarpone should be used in moderation. Low-fat crème fraîche, cottage cheese, and fromage frais can be used more frequently. Cottage cheese and other low-fat cheeses also add protein and make a smoothie more filling. They are good additions when a smoothie is being served in place of a full meal.

Ice Cream and sorbet:
These can be added to smoothies for extra creaminess or flavor, as well as to to cool the drink. They can be blended with the fruit or added by the scoop in place of ice.

Dairy substitutes: Tofu is high in protein and low in fat. It is a good source of calcium and contains vitamin E. It has little flavor but will give your drink a more satisfying thickness and creamy texture.

Soy milk and soy yogurt can also be used as an alternative to dairy products, as can rice milk and oat milk. You can also use coconut milk, banana, and avocado to give smoothies a creamy texture and good flavor.

Smoothie Hints and Tips

Recipes make one to two glasses, depending on the size of your glass and the amount you want to drink.

Stick to one type of measuring system. Never switch between them. Cup measurements are for standard American cups.

Wash fruit and vegetables well. Peel if required and cut into chunks.

Use fruit and vegetables in peak condition.

Prepare fruit and vegetables just before you need them. Some vitamins start to be destroyed as you cut into the produce, and some produce discolors quickly.

Add liquids such as fruit juice, milk, or yogurt to the blender first.

For maximum nutritional benefit, serve the drinks immediately after preparing them.

Smoothies may separate on standing. This does not affect the flavor. Serve with a straw twizzler or spoon to stir before drinking.

Fresh ripe fruit should provide enough natural sweetness, but you can add a little extra sugar or honey to sweeten if required.

Keep berries and chopped up soft fruit such as apricots, peaches, and bananas in the freezer to make instant iced smoothies. They can go into the blender when frozen.

Smoothies are best served cold. Chill the ingredients before use and serve with plenty of ice. Crushed ice will cool a drink quickly. You can also use ice cream or sorbet.

Smoothies tend to be thick, but you can alter the thickness of the drink to your taste. Simply add extra milk, water, or fruit juice to achieve your preferred thickness.

If the smoothie is too thin, add a banana, which is a great thickener, or some frozen ingredients such as frozen fruit or ice cream. Or use cooked rice to thicken the smoothie.

You can remove seeds, pips, or fibrous material from the smoothie by straining through a nylon sieve. This will remove the fibre content, thus affecting the nutritional value of the drink, but it is useful if you find them unpleasant or you have fussy children.

Some liquids increase in volume and froth on blending so never overfill the blender.

Make sure the lid is firmly on your blender before processing.

Wash the blender as soon as possible after use. If fruit becomes dried on, soak in warm soapy water for a few minutes to soften the fruit.

Equipment

Whether you want to make juices, smoothies, or both, there is certain equipment that will be essential to have in your kitchen.

Juices

If you want to make juice from hard fruit and vegetables such as carrots, apples, and pears, you will need to invest in a juicer. There are two main types of juicers available.

Centrifugal juicer: This is the least expensive type and it works by finely grating the fruit or vegetables and then spinning them at high speed to separate the juice from the pulp, which is then discarded.

Masticating juicer: This machine is more efficient, but it comes with a higher price tag. It finely chops the fruit, then forces the juice out through a fine mesh.

Food processor: Some types have a centrifugal juicer attachment. It will not be as efficient as a dedicated machine; however, it will be more than adequate for occasional juicing.

Citrus juicer: Citrus juicer attachments are available for some juicers and food processors. These are specifically designed to squeeze juice from citrus fruit and are the most efficient equipment for juicing this kind of fruit. However, you can squeeze citrus fruit by simply peeling and feeding the segments through the juicers. Alternatively, you may prefer to use a simple hand lemon squeezer or reamer.